T.R.
(TYRANNOSAURUS REX)
& FRIENDS

Written by
Rupert Matthews

Illustrated by
Tudor Humphries

DISCOVERY TOYS

Contents

Introduction

Dinosaurs were a group of reptiles that lived many millions of years ago, long before the earliest human beings. There were many different types, of all shapes and sizes. Most of them lived in North America, with others living in Europe, Africa and Asia.

The dinosaurs in this book lived at different times and in different places. Many of those shown are brightly colored, but in fact no one knows the true color of these extraordinary animals. Scientists' ideas about dinosaurs are constantly changing as new evidence is found.

Plant Eaters

Many types of dinosaurs ate plants. These dinosaurs usually had large, flat teeth and strong jaw muscles for chewing tough leaves and stems. **Tsintosaurus** ate twigs and pine needles. **Styracosaurus** had very sharp teeth, which some scientists think were used to chew tough palm fronds. Other dinosaurs ate softer foods, such as ferns, cycads and water plants.

Diplodocus
(dip-LOD-oh-kus)

Styracosaurus
(STY-rak-oh-SAW-rus)

Iguanodon
(ig-WA-no-DON)

Stegosaurus
(STEG-oh-SAW-rus)

Hypsilophodon
(hip-see-LOAF-oh-don)

Polacanthus
(POLL-a-CAN-thus)

Tsintosaurus
(SIN-tow-SAW-rus)

Hunters

Dinosaurs which ate other animals often had sharp teeth and claws for catching their prey. Large, strong meat-eating dinosaurs hunted other large dinosaurs. Smaller hunters caught such animals as lizards, insects and small mammals, and **Oviraptor** stole eggs.

Oviraptor
(OVE-ih-RAP-tor)

Velociraptor
(vel-O-si-RAP-tor)

Ceratosaurus
(SER-a-toe-SAW-rus)

Tyrannosaurus
(tie-RAN-oh-SAW-rus)

Allosaurus
(AL-oh-SAW-rus)

Coelurus
(seel-OO-rus)

Coelophysis
(seel-oh-FY-sis)

In the Air

Archaeopteryx is the earliest known bird. It lived about 150 million years ago and had teeth and a bony tail. Other flying animals which lived during the time of the dinosaurs were pterosaurs. They were covered in fur and had wings made of skin.

Quetzalcoatlus
(KWET-zal-co-AT-lus)

Rhamphorhynchus
(RAM-foe-RIN-kus)

Dimorphodon
(die-MORE-foe-don)

Archaeopteryx
are-kee-OP-tur-iks)
Pteranodon
(ter-AN-oh-don)
Pterodactylus
(TER-oh-DAK-til-us)

In the Oceans

Many reptiles lived in the ocean. **Placodus** lived near the bottom and ate shellfish found there. **Metriorhynchus** dived deep beneath the surface to catch fish. **Elasmosaurus** and **Plesiosaurus** lived near the surface, using their long necks to reach fish in the water. **Pliosaurus** could swim quickly to catch squid-like animals. **Ichthyosaurus** ate fish and could leap out of the water. **Archelon**, the largest turtle that ever existed, may have gone ashore to lay its eggs.

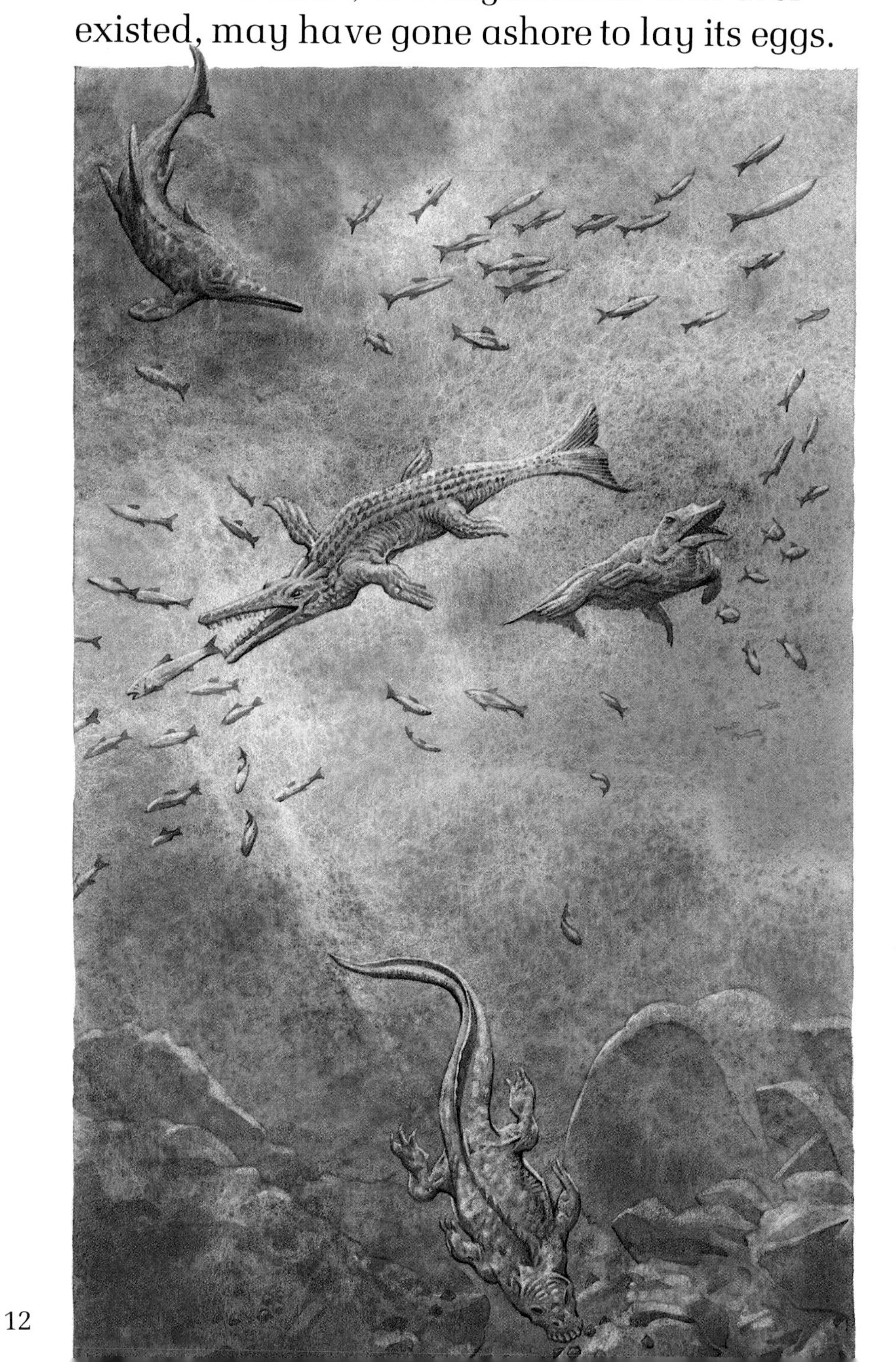

Placodus
(PLAK-oh-dus)

Metriorhynchus
(MET-ree-oh-RIN-ku

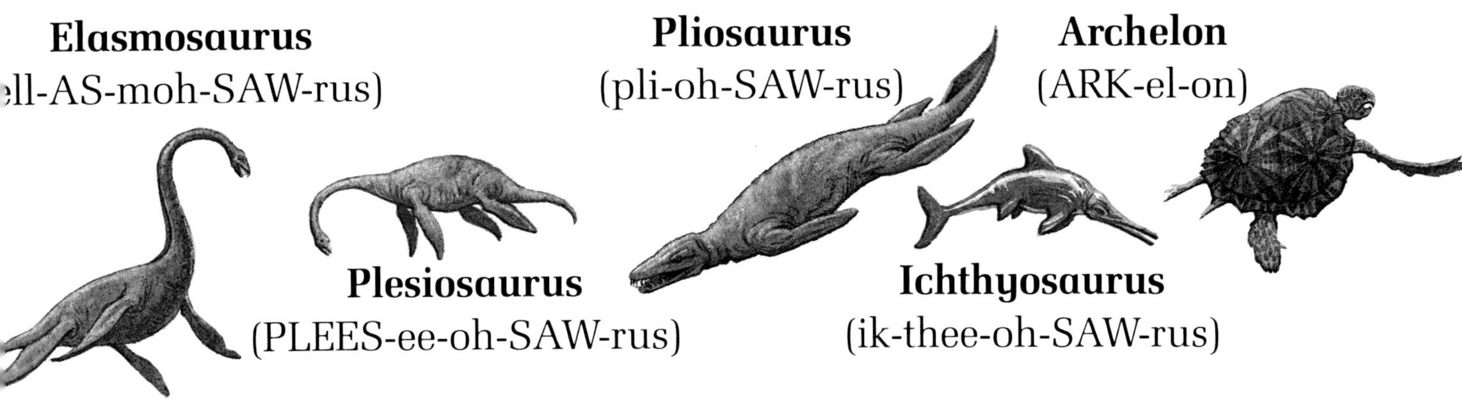
Elasmosaurus
ell-AS-moh-SAW-rus)
Pliosaurus
(pli-oh-SAW-rus)
Archelon
(ARK-el-on)
Plesiosaurus
(PLEES-ee-oh-SAW-rus)
Ichthyosaurus
(ik-thee-oh-SAW-rus)

Plodders

All these dinosaurs moved very slowly. The larger ones were protected from hunters by their size and strength. The smaller ones were protected by bony armor or sharp spikes. You can compare sizes in the top row of dinosaurs.

Diplodocus
(dip-LOD-oh-kus)
Cetiosaurus
(SEET-ee-oh-SAW-rus)
Ankylosaurus
(an-ky-low-SAW-rus)

Athletes

These dinosaurs were fast moving. Some hunters, such as **Deinonychus**, ran very quickly and leapt in the air to attack their prey. **Dryosaurus**, **Lesothosaurus** and other plant eaters ran at high speeds to escape from hunters. Two rival **Stegoceras** would have fought over food or territory by running at each other and butting their heads together. **Ornithomimus** and **Struthiomimus** were among the fastest of all the dinosaurs.

Deinonychus
(dy-NON-ee-kus)
Dryosaurus
(DRY-oh-SAW-rus)
Lesothosaurus
(LESS-oh-toe-SAW-rus)
Stegoceras
(steg-O-ser-as)
Ornithomimus
(OR-nith-oh-MY-mus)
Struthiomimus
(STROOTH-ee-oh-MIME-us)

Record Breakers

All dinosaurs were extraordinary in some way – but some were extraordinary even among themselves!

Ultrasaurus was the tallest of the dinosaurs. It stood 60 feet (18 meters) high.

Staurikosaurus was the earliest-known dinosaur.

Gallimimus
(GAL-ih-MIME-us)

Stenonychosaurus
(STEN-oh-NIKE-o-SAW-rus)

Compsognathus
(komp-sog-NATH-us)

The longest dinosaur was **Mamenchisaurus**, which measured 72 feet (22 meters).

Stenonychosaurus was probably the cleverest dinosaur. It used its intelligence to outwit small, fast prey.

The smallest dinosaur was **Compsognathus**, which was only 2 feet (60 centimeters) long.

Gallimimus was one of the fastest dinosaurs – it could run as quickly as the swiftest modern horse.

Ultrasaurus
(ULL-tra-SAW-rus)

Mamenchisaurus
ı-MENCH-ih-SAW-rus)

Staurikosaurus
tor-IK-oh-SAW-rus)

By looking in the box, you can see how small the dinosaurs on the left were in comparison to those above!

Dinosaur Dimensions

It is hard to imagine the actual size of the dinosaurs. But by comparing them with familiar objects, we can see just how big, or small, they really were.

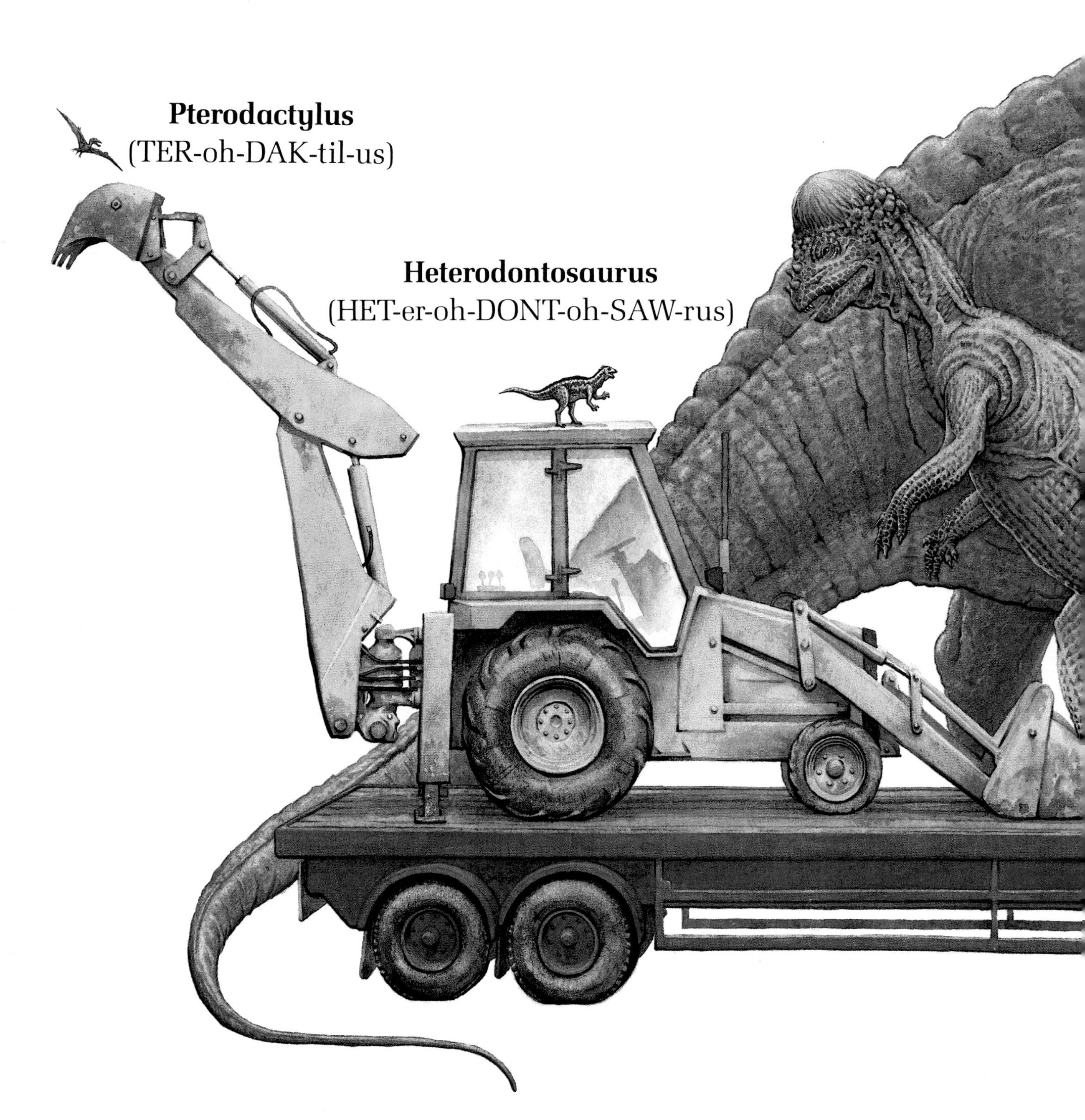

Pteranodon
(ter-AN-oh-don)
Apatosaurus
(a-PAT-oh-SAW-rus)
Pachycephalosaurus
(PAK-ee-KEF-al-oh-SAW-rus)
Coelurus
(seel-OO-rus)

Modern Parallels

Dinosaurs were very different from modern animals. But some dinosaurs lived and behaved in a similar way to animals we know today.

Albertosaurus
(al-BERT-oh-SAW-rus)

Triceratops
(try-SER-a-tops)

Saltasaurus
(SALT-a-SAW-rus)

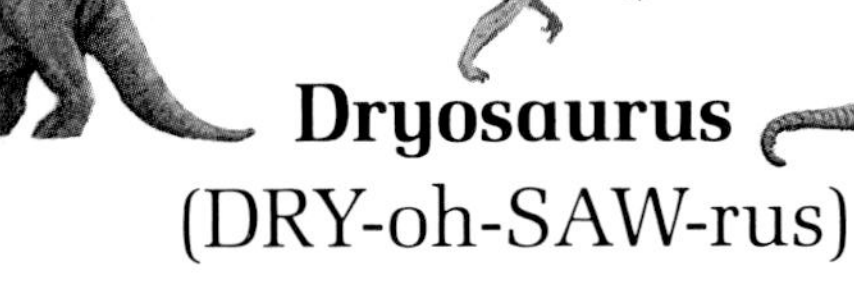

Ornitholestes
(or-NITH-oh-LESS-teez)

Dryosaurus
(DRY-oh-SAW-rus)

Can you match the dinosaurs to the modern animals and tell how they are similar? (See answers on page 28.)

Animals of the Dinosaur World

Many types of animals lived during the time of the dinosaurs. Some of these can still be seen today.
Can you name them? (See answers on page 29.)

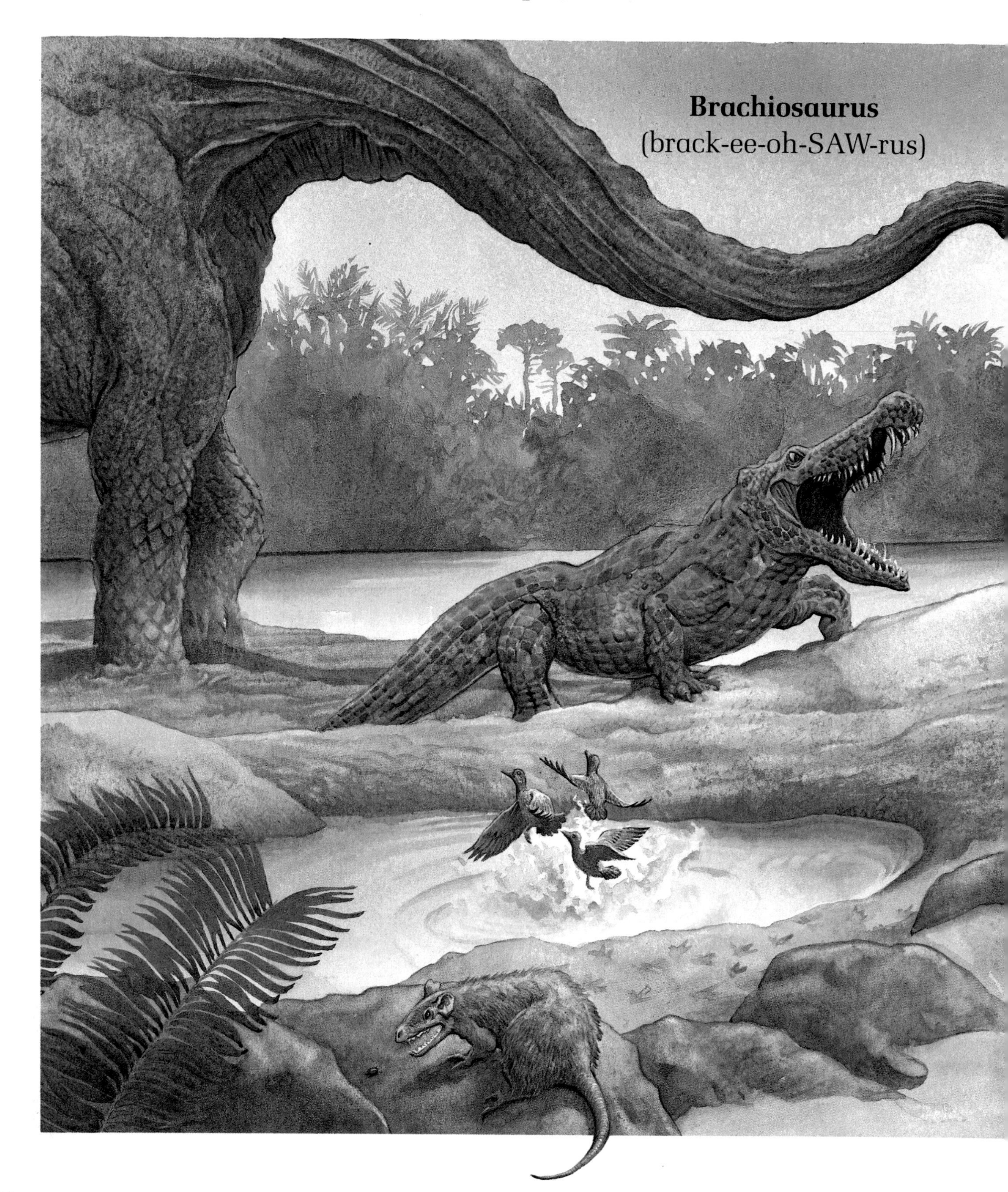

Parasaurolophus
(par-a-SAWR-oh-LOAF-us)

Dinosaur Fossils

Scientists know about dinosaurs by studying fossils, which are the remains of animals preserved in rock. Scientists dig fossils out of the ground. The fossils are then taken to museums, where they are examined by fossil specialists.

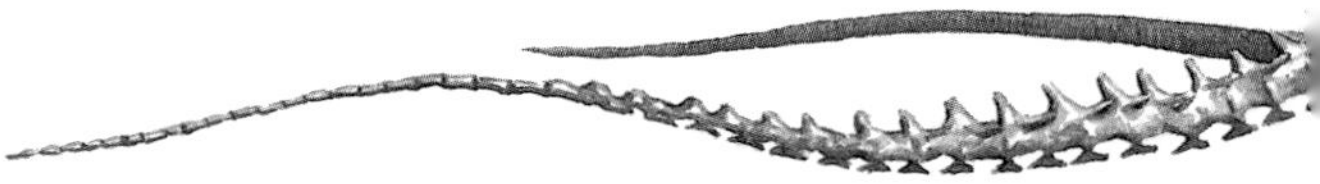

The most common type of fossil is fossilized bone. By building a skeleton out of these bones, scientists can create a picture of how the dinosaur looked when it was alive.

Some fossil skeletons are found together, such as this **Coelophysis** (right). This dinosaur had thin, light bones, which means that it was able to run quickly.

Not all fossils are bones. Sometimes fossilized nests and even eggs are found. From these we know that dinosaurs laid eggs and brought food to their young, just as birds do today. In some places, scientists have found fossilized dinosaur tracks. These have revealed how fast dinosaurs walked and ran.

Sometimes fossilized skeletons are found scattered in rock, as below. The task of putting these bones together requires much skill and patience. Because the fossils of this **Diplodocus** are large and strong, scientists know that the animal was big and moved slowly.

From the shape of its skull, scientists can tell that **Psittacosaurus** was related to such horned dinosaurs as Triceratops and Styracosaurus.

Answers

Modern Parallels (page 22)

Albertosaurus and the tiger are large, fierce hunters which attack other large animals.

Ornitholestes and the jackal hunt small animals, such as lizards and small mammals about the size of mice.

Triceratops and the rhinoceros eat plants and use their horns to defend themselves.

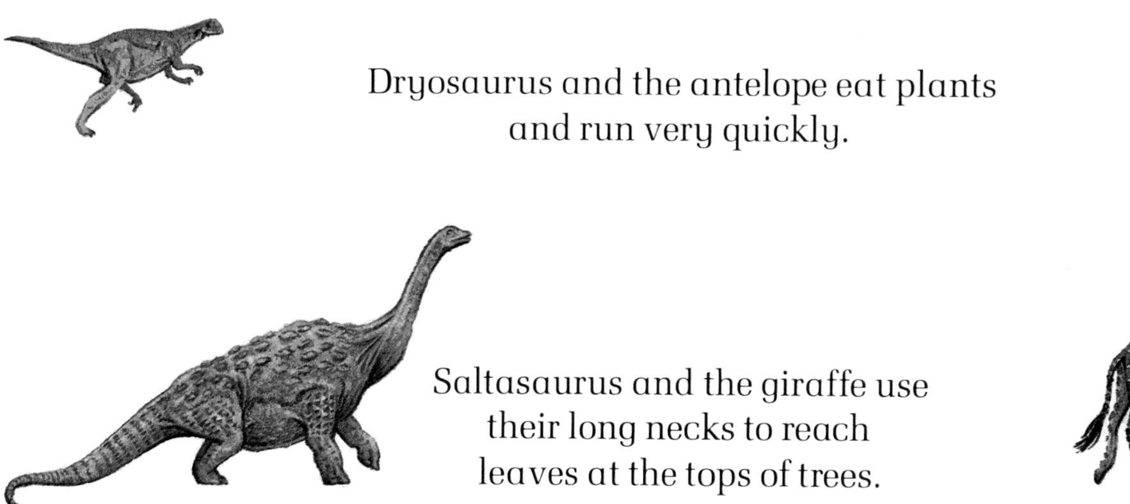

Dryosaurus and the antelope eat plants and run very quickly.

Saltasaurus and the giraffe use their long necks to reach leaves at the tops of trees.

Animals of the Dinosaur World (page 24)

Morganucodon was a mammal similar to the shrew.

Testudo was an early form of tortoise.

Madtsoia was a type of constricting snake. Poisonous snakes did not live at this time.

Leidyosuchus was a large crocodile.

There were also several types of birds, insects and lizards similar to those we find today.

Dinosaur Facts

Albertosaurus
"Alberta reptile"
26 feet (8 meters) long
lived 70 million years ago
in North America

Allosaurus
"foreign reptile"
35 feet (11 meters) long
lived 140 million years ago
in North America and Africa

Ankylosaurus
"stiff reptile"
33 feet (10 meters) long
lived 80 million years ago
in North America

Archaeopteryx
"ancient wing"
15 inches (40 centimeters) long
lived 150 million years ago
in Europe

Archelon
"ancient turtle"
13 feet (4 meters) long
lived 80 million years ago
in North America

Brachiosaurus
"arm reptile"
75 feet (23 meters) long
lived 150 million years ago
in North America and Africa

Ceratosaurus
"horned reptile"
20 feet (6 meters) long
lived 140 million years ago
in North America

Cetiosaurus
"whale reptile"
60 feet (18 meters) long
lived 160 million years ago
in Europe and Africa

Coelophysis
"hollow form"
10 feet (3 meters) long
lived 200 million years ago
in North America

Coelurus
"hollow tail"
7 feet (2 meters) long
lived 150 million years ago
in North America

Compsognathus
"pretty jaw"
2 feet (60 centimeters) long
lived 150 million years ago
in Europe

Deinonychus
"terrible claw"
13 feet (4 meters) long
lived 120 million years ago
in North America

Dimorphodon
"two forms of tooth"
13 feet (4 meters) long
lived 120 million years ago
in North America

Diplodocus
"two-ridged reptile"
90 feet (27 meters) long
lived 140 million years ago
in North America

Dryosaurus
"oak lizard"
14 feet (4.3 meters) long
lived 150 million years ago
in North America and Europe

Elasmosaurus
"ribbon reptile"
43 feet (13 meters) long
lived 80 million years ago
in North America

Gallimimus
"hen mimic"
13 feet (4 meters) long
lived 80 million years ago
in Asia

Hylaeosaurus
"woodland lizard"
20 feet (6 meters) long
lived 120 million years ago
in Europe

Hypsilophodon
"high-ridge tooth"
7.5 feet (2.3 meters) long
lived 120 million years ago
in Europe and North America

Ichthyosaurus
"fish lizard"
16 feet (5 meters) long
lived 140 million years ago
in Europe

Iguanodon
"iguana tooth"
26 feet (8 meters) long
lived 120 million years ago
in Europe

Kentrosaurus
"pointed lizard"
16 feet (5 meters) long
lived 140 million years ago
in Africa

Lesothosaurus
"reptile from Lesotho"
3 feet (1 meter) long
lived 200 million years ago
in Africa

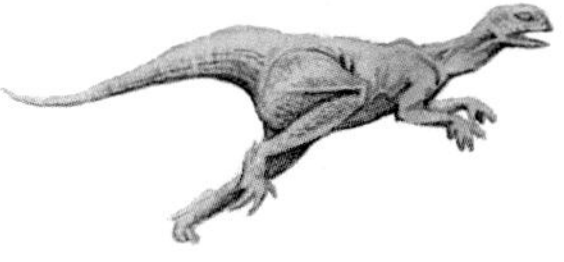

Mamenchisaurus
"Mamenchin (China) reptile"
72 feet (22 meters) long
lived 150 million years ago
in Asia